S0-AJR-031

DATE DUE

NOV 9 1990			
DEC 5 - 1990			
JAN 8 1991 JAN 8 1991			

NORTH COUNTY SCHOOL DISTRICT
500 SPRING GROVE ROAD
HOLLISTER, CALIFORNIA 95023

DEMCO

AIRPORTS

GRAHAM RICKARD

The Bookwright Press
New York · 1987

Topics

All the words that appear
in **bold** are explained in the
glossary on page 30

Cover photograph: Dusseldorf Airport, Germ

First published in the
United States in 1987 by
The Bookwright Press
387 Park Avenue South
New York, NY 10016

First published in 1986 by
Wayland (Publishers) Ltd
61 Western Road, Hove
East Sussex, BN3 1JD, England

Phototypeset by
Kalligraphics Ltd
Redhill, Surrey, England
Printed in Belgium by
Casterman

© Copyright 1986 Wayland (Publishers) Ltd

ISBN 0–531–18142–1   T2614

Library of Congress Catalog Card Number: 86–72829

Contents

What Are Airports?

Just as ships need harbors, and trains need stations, so aircraft need airports. Here, they can collect and unload their passengers and cargoes, be refueled, **serviced**, and take off and land. Since the Wright brothers' first experimental flights in the 1900s, flying has become the fastest-growing industry of this century. Millions of people every year now take to the skies. The constant growth in

There are many small airports today used only by light aircraft. This one is in Mauritania.

demand for air travel means that larger aircraft and more airports are always needed. There are now about 800 major international airports throughout the world, and many thousands of smaller ones used by light planes.

Early aircraft were small and light, and needed only a flat grass runway to take off and land. When London's Heathrow Airport first opened in 1945, it had one short runway, a small control room, and a collection of tents and trailers as its passenger lounge. Now it is the

Some planes need only a grass runway, like this one in Nepal, to take off and land.

Busy airports, like Kuwait International, have to cope with thousands of passengers every hour.

world's busiest international airport, with four separate **terminals**, handling 26 million passengers and over 270,000 aircraft movements every year. That's more than one take off or landing every minute!

Many modern airports employ thousands of people to look after the airlines' passengers and aircraft. They are like miniature towns, with their own roads, hotels, churches, stores, hospitals, police and firefighters. Large jumbo **jets** can carry up to 500 passengers at a time, so all the airport facilities have to be carefully organized to provide an efficient 24-hour service for the thousands of passengers who pass through the terminals every hour.

For tired travelers, airports are usually places to leave as quickly as possible, and for those who live nearby they are often a noisy nuisance. But they are also interesting places, often busy and full of people, and there are many exciting things to see.

This clock at Singapore Airport tells passengers what time it is in different parts of the world.

The Airport Buildings

The most important part of an airport is the runway, which aircraft use for taking off and landing. Large modern jets can weigh over 370 tons and land at speeds over 270 kph (167 mph). They need long runways with a hard surface, to take their weight.

The lights help to guide the pilot onto the runway.

Most international airports have more than one runway. One of the world's longest runways, at 4,615m (15,140ft) is at Doha Airport in the Persian Gulf.

A system of colored lights on the runway helps pilots to land the plane at night or in bad weather. Red and white approach lights guide the pilot to the end of the runway, which is marked by a line of green lights, while the runway itself is lit by amber lights.

Between the runway and the airport buildings, **taxiways** lead to the flat concrete area called the **apron**, where the aircraft stand to load and unload their passengers. The arriving aircraft are guided to their parking places by people called ramp agents, who wave brightly colored reflectors.

All aircraft movements are controlled by the air control staff in the control tower. They use electronic equipment to plot and

The ramp agent directs the plane to its parking place.

The inside of the control tower at Riyadh Airport.

continually check the exact position of the dozens of aircraft that are waiting to use the airfield at any one time. At a busy airport, this can be very complicated to organize! The control tower is the nerve center of the whole airport, and no pilot can land or take off without the permission of the control staff.

Below the control tower are the terminal buildings, which passengers use when boarding or leaving the aircraft. In the terminal buildings, only passengers who have gone through passport and **security** checks are allowed to board their planes. Because they have to accommodate so many travelers, some terminal buildings are really vast.

Behind the terminals there are storage areas for fuel, cargo warehouses, aircraft service **hangars**, and the airlines' food kitchens. Because most airports are quite a long way from the nearest city, transportation to and from them is very important.

The Haji Terminal at King Abd al-Aziz Airport near Jeddah is the world's largest roofed structure. It covers 1.5 sq km. (nearly 4 sq mi).

Servicing Aircraft

Refueling planes is an important part of the work at an airport.

As soon as a plane **taxies** onto the apron the ground crew go into action to give the plane a quick "turnaround" time, so that it can take off again as soon as possible. A special truck pumps fuel from underground pipes into the aircraft fuel tanks. A jumbo jet flying

Loading cargo onto a waiting plane at Tel Aviv Airport.

across the Atlantic from Europe to America uses about 120 tons of fuel, but its tanks can be filled in just twenty minutes.

Separate crews empty the toilets and clean the plane. Engineers check the aircraft's engines, tires, brakes, lights and electrical systems. Cargo and **duty-free goods** are loaded for the next flight.

Airport kitchens prepare meals to be served during flights.

The kitchen areas of the plane are restocked with pre-cooked meals from the airline's kitchens, or from independent catering services. Major airlines each serve about 11 million meals a year.

Constant checks help to make flying one of the safest ways to travel, but accidents do sometimes happen. Most occur on take off or landing, and all airports have emergency services on constant standby. If an aircraft does crash, it may catch fire and burn very fast because of its large fuel tanks. The firefighters have to control the fire very quickly. A special fire engine that can travel very fast over rough ground, can carry enough foam to keep a fire under control until the larger rescue vehicles arrive.

Nature also provides her own dangers at airports. A flock of birds can crack an aircraft's windshield or, if sucked into a jet, can easily cause engine failure.

An airport firefighter practices to be ready in case of an emergency.

A snow blower clears the runway of Aberdeen Airport in Scotland.

Many airports use sirens or fireworks to scare birds off the runways and to keep the air approaches clear. Bad weather conditions such as snow and fog can also create serious problems, and may even close an airport. For example, even a 2 cm (1 in) covering at a major airport means that thousands of tons of snow has to be removed in order to keep the airport open.

Looking After Passengers

When passengers arrive at the terminal, they make their way first to the check-in desks to show their tickets, obtain **boarding passes** and leave their luggage. Passengers are allowed to carry a small amount of hand luggage on the plane, but larger items are weighed, labeled, and put on a **conveyor belt** leading to the baggage-handling area.

A check-in desk at Melbourne Airport in Australia.

Here, handlers sort the bags onto the waiting planes, where they are loaded into the **hold**. Near the check-in desks there are banks for changing foreign money, stores, restaurants, toilets and other facilities. In large airports there are television screens or boards giving up-to-date information about the flights. Because so many people from different countries pass through airports, the loudspeaker announcements are often in several languages.

Duty-free shops sell goods at low prices.

Passengers with boarding passes go to the departure lounge once they have gone though the **customs** check and shown their passports. Here they wait for their flights, and visit the duty-free shops, which sell goods such as spirits and perfumes and cameras at low prices.

When the flight is announced, passengers pass through a final **security scan**, which will show up any suspicious objects, such as weapons hidden in hand luggage or clothing. Different airports use

A security scan can show up any hidden weapons.

At this airport, in the U.S.S.R., passengers walk to the aircraft.

different methods for moving passengers from the terminal to the plane. Many airports use mobile corridors leading from the departure lounge, but at Jeddah Airport the lounge itself is on wheeled stilts and the whole room moves to the aircraft for the passengers to board the plane.

When they land at their destination, travelers are taken to the arrivals lounge, where they collect their luggage. Usually, the bags keep going around on a conveyor belt, until their owner recognizes them and picks them up. Then passengers arriving from abroad go through the passport control area and on to the customs control checkpoint.

Airports have medical centers staffed by doctors and nurses and many also have an animal shelter run by skilled staff, to look after any four-legged passengers. Permanent police teams and security forces protect the airport and its customers against crime and the increasing threat of attacks by terrorists.

Passengers on international flights have their passports checked before they can board their flight.

Airports Large and Small

Airports can be in very remote areas, like this one in Alaska.

Not all airports have long runways or large terminal buildings handling hundreds of international flights every day. There are many thousands of small airstrips throughout the world that provide a safe, if bumpy, landing for small light aircraft. In many remote areas

aircraft provide the main contact with the outside world, and are the only way of delivering mail and medical supplies. The famous "Flying Doctor" service in Australia shows just how useful such airstrips can be.

The Australian "Flying Doctor" lands on an airstrip at an Aboriginal settlement in the Northern Territory.

These planes can take off and land on water.

Some planes are fitted with floats or skis, for landings on water or snow, and **jump jets** need no runway at all. Aircraft carriers, the largest ships in modern navies, are really massive floating airports, which can travel to wherever they are needed. Some can carry up to 100 aircraft.

Helicopters need only a launch pad, rather than a runway, so they can be very useful in places where space is limited, such as on oil rigs. Helicopters have many other uses, such as ferrying passengers between airports.

America boasts the world's busiest airport for **domestic flights**. Chicago's O'Hare Field Airport handles 670,000 aircraft movements and 43 million passengers a year.

Helicopters need only a small space for landing.

Dallas and Fort Worth Airport in Texas, will soon be the world's largest airport, with 9 runways and 14 terminals. Lhasa Airport in Tibet is the highest in the world, at 4,363m, (14,313ft) above sea level, while Schiphol, Amsterdam, at 3.9m (12ft) below sea level, is the lowest.

Most airports have an untidy, unfinished look about them, because they are constantly being altered and enlarged to keep pace with the demand for air travel,

The airport at Riyadh was designed with passengers' comfort in mind.

which roughly doubles every five years! This may affect those who have to live and work near the airports. Large modern jets cause air and noise **pollution**, which can seriously affect the lives of people living in areas where planes fly at a low level, or take off and land. In some places, airport authorities try to help local people by giving them money toward the cost of making their homes more soundproof, and by trying to restrict the number of night flights. However, as the demand for air travel increases, pollution may well get worse in the future.

Aircraft noise at night may disturb people's sleep if they live near an airport.

A number of airports are being built throughout the world, and the planners are constantly searching for new ways to make airports better and more acceptable to those who live nearby. Soon, we will need a whole new generation of airports to handle flights on new, more advanced aircraft.

It has been suggested that airports of the future should be built well away from major residential areas. One answer would be to

Different aircraft require varying amounts of space to take off and land.

build airports on vast inflatable platforms, which would float on the surface of the ocean, cutting out the need to use large areas of valuable farming land, and sparing residents the nuisance of aircraft noise and pollution.

We can be sure that the airports of the future will be even larger and more advanced than the ones that we have today.

It is likely that airports of the future will be even larger than those we know today.

Glossary

Apron The concrete area between the runway and terminal building, used to load and unload planes after landing and before take off.

Boarding pass The ticket that allows passengers to get on the plane.

Conveyor belt A continuous moving strip of material that carries things from one point to another.

Customs The point where luggage is examined to prevent smuggling of goods.

Domestic flights Flights within one country. Flights going abroad are international.

Duty-free goods Goods on which there is no government tax.

Hangar A large shed for housing and servicing aircraft.

Hold The large part of an aircraft's body, used for carrying cargo and passengers' luggage.

Jets Planes driven by the power of hot air forced out of the rear.

Jump jets Jet planes that can take off and land without needing a runway.

Pollution The fumes and the noise that the aircraft makes.

Security Making sure a place is safe and well protected.

Security scan An electronic device that checks for hidden objects.

To Service To look after and keep in working order.

Taxiway The route between the runway and apron, used by aircraft to move around the airport before take off or after landing.

Terminals The places where planes pick up and leave passengers.

To taxi To move slowly along the ground. (Used of aircraft).

Books to Read

Aiports by David Peterson
    (Children Press, 1981)
Airports by Michael Jay and Mark
    Hewish (Franklin Watts, 1982)
Careers with an Airline by Jennifer
    B. Dean (Lerner Publications,
    1973)
In the Air by Eugene Booth
    (Raintree, 1977)
*The Story of the Flight at Kitty
    Hawk* by Conrad R. Stein
    (Children Press, 1981)
What it's Like to be a Pilot by
    Arthur Shay (Contemporary
    Books, 1971)

Picture Acknowledgments

The illustrations in this book were supplied by: British Airports Authority 18 (Gatwick Airport); Camerapix 21; Hutchinson Picture Library 4 (Mauritania), 6 (Kuwait Airport), 10, 25 (North Sea oil rig), 26 (Riyadh Airport); Tony Morrison, South American Pictures 28 (Ecuador Airport); Photri USA 19, 29 (Los Angeles Airport); John Topham Picture Library 7, 11, 15 (Manston Airport), 27 (Dubai Airport); Victorian Tourism Commission, Australia 17 (Tullamarine Airport, Melbourne); Wayland Picture Library 23, ZEFA 5 (Nepal Airport), 8, 9 (Dusseldorf Airport), 12, 13 (Ben Gurion Airport), 14, 16 (Aberdeen Airport), 20 (USSR), 22, 24 (Peru).

Index